With this Ring...

BOOKMARK
PUBLISHING GROUP

ISBN: I-894637-0I-I

Bookmark Publishing Group
100 Lombard Street
Suite 103
Toronto, Ontario
Canada
M5C 1M3

Publisher: Susan Yates
Writers: Sally Beals, Eva Blank
Editorial Services: Colborne Communications
Text and Cover Design: Dave Murphy/ArtPlus Ltd.
Page Layout: Leanne O'Brien/ArtPlus Ltd.
Cover Photo: Nasuko/Photonica

Developed and produced exclusively for Avalon Music.

Avalon Music
250 Ferrand Drive
Suite 1100
Toronto, ON
M3C 3G8

Printed and bound in Canada

TABLE OF CONTENTS

Wedding Bells will Ring   5

Making Plans   9

The Wedding Party   21

The Honour of Your Presence   27

Unique Invitations   37

Your Wish List   43

A Best-Dressed Wedding   49

Sweet Sounds   59

The Wedding Feast   67

The Beauty of Flowers   75

Picture Perfect   85

Pre-Wedding Parties   93

Ceremony Celebrations   101

Reception Ready   115

Saying "Thank You"   123

If ever two were one, then surely we.

If ever man were loved by wife, then thee.

ANNE BRADSTREET

WEDDING BELLS
WILL RING

Congratulations—you're engaged! This is a wonderful time of life, so take a deep breath and enjoy every minute of it.

The word "engaged" is actually part of the phrase "engaged to be married," and as such, it implies planning: a joyful time for both organization and wish-making. Share your dreams, and enlist the help of your loved ones for a wedding day to remember forever.

Yes, there will be a lot to do. That's why it is essential for you to keep the larger picture in mind. The engagement period is a time for friendship and family, for spending time with your fiancé, and—most importantly—for celebrating. After all, this is the beginning of your new life with your husband-to-be. You will receive gifts, words of love and congratulations, and visits from all those you hold dear. Everyone will want to see your ring, hear the romantic stories of the proposal, and raise a glass in your honor. Through all of it, have a marvelous time, because this is your party.

The wedding, throughout the ages, has been subject to all manner of traditions, customs, superstitions, and friendly pieces of advice. It is for this reason that you will need to know what your choices are and how to narrow them down. From early budgeting and planning to the moment you climb into your "just-married" carriage, this book offers you words of help, inspiration, and solace. Handy tips, checklists, journal pages, and origins of wedding traditions and superstitions are included to get you through this exciting and busy time.

Remember, above all else, your engagement is a time to take strength and joy from your love, follow your heart, and plan a day that's memorable for a lifetime.

The wedding band, a circle unbroken, symbolizes eternal love. Before the sixteenth century, brides decorated their wrists and ankles with circles of braided grass: the early form of today's wedding ring. The ring is worn on the left hand on the third finger (the thumb doesn't count as a finger). Traditionally, it was believed that the vein of love (vena amoris) ran from the ring finger directly to the heart, so your ring keeps your true love close to your heart.

Love conquers all things:

let us too give in to Love.

VIRGIL

To love someone deeply gives you strength.

Being loved by someone deeply gives you courage.

LAO TZU

MAKING PLANS

Behind every perfect wedding is a lot of level-headed and careful planning. And so there should be—your wedding day will be one of the most unforgettable days in your lives. Though all of the details may seem overwhelming at first, everything will start to fall into place if you take the planning step by step. Use this chapter to help you along the way as you put together a stunning marriage celebration.

As you prepare for your wedding, you will probably enlist a whole team of professionals—caterers, florists, musicians, jewellers—to help you orchestrate the occasion. And with all of those professionals comes a lot of paperwork.

That's why it can be really useful to put together a "wedding organizer" right at the beginning, so that you can file away important contracts and documents as you get them. You might want to consider an accordion file with different sections or a large binder with dividers (for this option, however, you will also need a hole punch!).

Whichever method you choose, start by labeling the sections of your organizer to hold papers for the different aspects of your wedding—such as "Catering," "Flowers," and "Music." File everything that you can, including contact information, notes taken from telephone conversations, written estimates, and contracts. Take the organizer with you when you do any wedding errands. This way, when your caterer asks for the specifications of the banquet hall, you can give her the phone number of the person with whom you booked the reception site.

Did you know that gold rings were at one time used for currency? If a man gave his sweetheart a gold ring, then, according to Roman law, she was assured security. The diamond became a popular choice for rings in the nineteenth century since it was called the Venus stone, after the goddess of love.

PRE-WEDDING CHECKLIST

12 months prior to the wedding

- Determine the date of your wedding.
- Determine the reception site. In the case of an outdoor wedding, decide on plans in case of inclement weather.
- Decide on the size and formality of the event.

11 months prior to the wedding

- Decide on a budget for your wedding.
- Determine the ceremony site. In the case of an outdoor wedding, decide on plans in case of inclement weather.
- If you choose, mail an engagement picture to your hometown newspaper.

10 months prior to the wedding

- Begin speaking with photographers, videographers, musicians, and florists to make necessary arrangements.
- Begin shopping for your dress, headpiece, and veil.

9 months prior to the wedding

- Meet with your officiant and, if required as part of a religious wedding, book pre-wedding counseling appointments.
- Decide on your wedding attendants.

8 months prior to the wedding

- Choose and order your invitations.
- Meet with your caterer to begin planning your menu.

7 months prior to the wedding

- Decide on the attire for your attendants.
- Select your honeymoon locale, and speak to a travel agent if necessary.

6 months prior to the wedding

- Register for your wedding gifts.
- Bring dress swatches to your florist to match colors.

5 months prior to the wedding

○ Choose your wedding rings and arrange for engraving.

○ Choose and order your wedding cake.

4 months prior to the wedding

○ Choose, and get written contracts from, your musicians for the ceremony and your band or deejay for the reception.

○ Address your wedding invitations (remember to include maps or directions for out-of-town guests).

○ Organize a program for the wedding.

○ Buy a wedding guest book.

3 months prior to the wedding

○ Hire limousines for the wedding day.

○ Book your honeymoon.

○ Confirm the menu with your caterer.

○ Meet with singers/musicians and confirm details regarding the music. Get this all in writing.

○ Arrange transportation to and from the wedding.

2 months prior to the wedding

○ Decide on your going-away clothes or clothes for the remainder of the wedding day.

○ Mail your wedding invitations.

○ Select party favors for your guests.

○ Begin thinking about your cake top. Discuss ideas with your baker.

1 month prior to the wedding

○ Make a list of photographs you want taken during your wedding. Give this list to your photographer.

○ Discuss bachelor/ette parties. Arrange for these to happen about a week before the wedding day.

○ Have a final fitting of your gown.

○ Call your caterer with a reasonable estimate of exactly how many people will be attending. Review the caterer's duties, as well as those of the wait staff.

○ Ensure that the cake has been ordered.

○ Confirm with your florist that everything has been ordered, and will be delivered at the time and date specified.

○ Select the groom's wedding gift.

- Make a seating plan if you would like one. Decide who will be in the receiving line. Write out place cards, if desired.

2 weeks prior to the wedding

- Choose a day for you and your fiancé to obtain a marriage license.
- Make a last check that clothing for everyone in the bridal party is in order.
- If you are changing your name, arrange for an altered bank account, Social Security Number, Driver's License, and so on.
- Make arrangements to transport gifts from rehearsal dinner location to wedding location.
- Give cards or small gifts to anyone who has given extra help with planning.
- Complete wedding announcement forms to send in to your hometown newspaper.

1 week prior to the wedding

- Finalize rehearsal dinner plans.
- Wrap all gifts to be given after the rehearsal dinner.
- Begin packing for your honeymoon.
- Make final calls to your photographer, videographer, officiant, musicians/singers, and florist.

1 day prior to the wedding

- Treat yourself to a pedicure, manicure, and massage to help you relax.
- Attend rehearsal dinner and review responsibilities one last time.
- Give seating arrangements to ushers and anyone else involved in seating guests.

The wedding day

- Take time to relax in a warm bath.
- Give yourself at least two hours to dress.

THE WEDDING BUDGET

Use this budgeting table to work out your wedding costs.

Ceremony/Reception Site

Item	Estimate #1	Estimate #2	Actual Cost
Ceremony site rental	$ _____	$ _____	$ _____
Officiant's fee	$ _____	$ _____	$ _____
Reception site rental	$ _____	$ _____	$ _____
Other _____	$ _____	$ _____	$ _____
TOTAL	$ _____	$ _____	$ _____

Stationery

Item	Estimate #1	Estimate #2	Actual Cost
Invitations	$ _____	$ _____	$ _____
Thank-you notes	$ _____	$ _____	$ _____
Personalized napkins, place cards, etc.	$ _____	$ _____	$ _____
Announcements	$ _____	$ _____	$ _____
Other _____	$ _____	$ _____	$ _____
TOTAL	$ _____	$ _____	$ _____

Music

Item	Estimate #1	Estimate #2	Actual Cost
Musicians for ceremony	$ _____	$ _____	$ _____
Band/deejay for reception	$ _____	$ _____	$ _____
Other _____	$ _____	$ _____	$ _____
TOTAL	$ _____	$ _____	$ _____

Catering

Item	Estimate #1	Estimate #2	Actual Cost
Pre-wedding parties	$ _____	$ _____	$ _____
Reception	$ _____	$ _____	$ _____
Liquor	$ _____	$ _____	$ _____
Wedding cake	$ _____	$ _____	$ _____
Bartender/wait staff	$ _____	$ _____	$ _____
Other _____	$ _____	$ _____	$ _____
TOTAL	$ _____	$ _____	$ _____

Photography/Videography

Item	Estimate #1	Estimate #2	Actual Cost
Formal portraits	$ _____	$ _____	$ _____
Extra prints	$ _____	$ _____	$ _____
Videotape	$ _____	$ _____	$ _____
Other _____	$ _____	$ _____	$ _____
TOTAL	$ _____	$ _____	$ _____

Bridal Attire

Item	Estimate #1	Estimate #2	Actual Cost
Dress	$ _____	$ _____	$ _____
Shoes	$ _____	$ _____	$ _____
Jewelry	$ _____	$ _____	$ _____
Headpiece and veil	$ _____	$ _____	$ _____
Other _____	$ _____	$ _____	$ _____
TOTAL	$ _____	$ _____	$ _____

Groom's Attire

Item	Estimate #1	Estimate #2	Actual Cost
Suit/tuxedo	$ _____	$ _____	$ _____
Shoes	$ _____	$ _____	$ _____
Shirt and tie	$ _____	$ _____	$ _____
Other _____	$ _____	$ _____	$ _____
TOTAL	**$** _____	**$** _____	**$** _____

Gifts

Item	Estimate #1	Estimate #2	Actual Cost
Attendants	$ _____	$ _____	$ _____
Groom	$ _____	$ _____	$ _____
Parents	$ _____	$ _____	$ _____
Other _____	$ _____	$ _____	$ _____
TOTAL	**$** _____	**$** _____	**$** _____

Flowers

Item	Estimate #1	Estimate #2	Actual Cost
Reception	$ _____	$ _____	$ _____
Ceremony	$ _____	$ _____	$ _____
Bridal bouquet	$ _____	$ _____	$ _____
Table decorations	$ _____	$ _____	$ _____
Other _____	$ _____	$ _____	$ _____
TOTAL	**$** _____	**$** _____	**$** _____

Transportation

Item	Estimate #1	Estimate #2	Actual Cost
Limousine or car	$ _____	$ _____	$ _____
Parking	$ _____	$ _____	$ _____
Valet services	$ _____	$ _____	$ _____
Other _____	$ _____	$ _____	$ _____
TOTAL	$ _____	$ _____	$ _____

Other Necessary Items

Item	Estimate #1	Estimate #2	Actual Cost
Wedding rings	$ _____	$ _____	$ _____
Ceremony assistants	$ _____	$ _____	$ _____
Wedding consultant/ coordinator	$ _____	$ _____	$ _____
Other _____	$ _____	$ _____	$ _____
TOTAL	$ _____	$ _____	$ _____

Total Cost

Estimate #1	Estimate #2	Actual Cost
$ _____	$ _____	$ _____

ALL IN THE FAMILY:
PAYMENT RESPONSIBILITIES

As you and the groom plan each aspect of your wedding day, you may be wondering: who is supposed to pay for what? Use these outlines for weddings both traditional and modern as you decide who foots the bill.

Traditional sharing of expenses

The bride and her family

- Groom's wedding ring and gift
- Gifts for bride's attendants
- Accommodation for attendants from out of town
- All reception costs
- Bride's wedding attire

- All stationery costs (invitations, thank-you notes, announcements)
- Bridesmaid's bouquets
- Ceremony costs: rental of site, musicians' fees, decoration
- Transportation for wedding party to and from ceremony and reception
- Photography costs

A Wedding Invitation

The groom and his family

- Bride's wedding ring and gift
- Officiant's fee
- The honeymoon
- Gifts for groom's best man/attendant and ushers
- Rehearsal dinner

Modern sharing of expenses

The bride's family

- Ceremony costs: the site fee and music
- Reception costs: site rental and catering
- The wedding cake and groom's cake

The groom's family

- Reception costs: liquor and beverages, music
- Photography/videography
- Transportation for wedding party to and from ceremony and reception

The bride and groom

- Attire for bride and groom
- Wedding rings
- Gifts for attendants
- All flowers
- All stationery costs (invitations, thank-you notes, announcements)

Who, being loved, is poor?

OSCAR WILDE

If love were what the rose is,

And I were like the leaf,

Our lives would grow together

In sad or singing weather.

ALGERNON CHARLES SWINBURNE

THE WEDDING
PARTY

On your wedding day, you will want to share your happiness with those closest to you in your life. And as expertly as you may plan this important day, you will also need some help. This is where your wedding party comes in.

Your attendants are there to support you on your big day. Following are some guidelines about their responsibilities.

Maid or matron of honor

This should be your closest confidante. Her role, in general, is to support the bride in whatever she can, from shopping for dresses to helping with honeymoon arrangements. Specifically, here are her duties:

- She is generally expected to host a bridal shower.
- She should be available to attend all pre-wedding functions.
- She might help arrange the purchase of small gifts for other wedding helpers.
- On your wedding day, she will help you get dressed and finish packing your going-away clothes.
- In the ceremony, she holds the groom's ring and the bride's bouquet, adjusts your veil and train, and signs your marriage license as a witness.

> ### BRIDE'S HELPER
> If your closest confidante happens to be male, or the groom's best friend is female, don't worry. Instead of having a maid of honor or a best man, it is now quite common to have an "honor attendant" of the opposite sex who fulfills all of the traditional functions.

- During the reception, she offers a toast to the happy couple.

Best man

This will probably be your groom's dearest friend, but he could also be a brother, father, or other close relative. He is the counterpoint to the maid of honor, and his job is to assist the groom in whatever emergency tasks need doing. Here are his specific responsibilities:

- If the groom is having a men-only pre-wedding party, the best man hosts it.
- He makes sure that the groom and the ushers get to the ceremony site on time.
- He holds checks for the clergy and musicians.
- He holds the bride's ring during the ceremony.
- He signs the marriage license as a witness.
- At the reception, he makes the first toast to the bride and groom and reads any telegrams that were sent.

Bridesmaids

If you are having a small and simple wedding, you may choose to only have a maid of honor. For larger weddings, it is traditional to also appoint bridesmaids. This is generally what they are expected to do:

- To help the bride with various pre-wedding errands, such as addressing invitations and picking up last-minute supplies.
- To co-host a shower or throw a bachelorette party.

Ushers

Generally, you and the groom should appoint one usher for every fifty guests. You and the groom together should choose a head usher, perhaps a close and responsible friend or relative. Here are the responsibilities of the ushers:

- The head usher will be in charge of ensuring that any other ushers arrive at the ceremony site on time, and will also escort the bride and groom's mothers to their seats.
- The ushers will be present at the men-only pre-wedding party.

- The ushers will escort guests to their appropriate places.

Ring bearer

If there is a boy between four and eight years of age in your close family or circle of friends, why not ask him to be your ring bearer? He'll make a charming addition to any wedding party. Here is his responsibility:

- To carry symbolic rings, pinned or tied to a satin pillow, down the aisle.

Flower girl

The flower girl, also between the ages of four and eight, is usually second only to the bride in appreciative sighs and murmurs from guests during the processional. Here is her responsibility:

- To precede the bride in the processional, strewing flower petals on the ground from a small basket to ensure that you tread on a beauteous path. You can update this tradition by giving the flower girl a simple bouquet to carry.

BRIDE'S HELPER

What a relief! Your wedding party is expected to pay for all of their own travel and clothing costs.

THE WEDDING PARTY

Maid/Matron of Honor or Honor Attendant

_____

Relation to Bride

_____

Best Man or Honor Attendant

_____

Relation to Groom

_____

Bridesmaids

_____

_____

_____

_____

Relation to Bride/Groom

_____

_____

_____

_____

Ushers

_____

_____

_____

_____

Relation to Bride/Groom

_____

_____

_____

_____

Ring Bearer

_____

Relation to Bride/Groom

_____

Flower Girl

_____

Relation to Bride/Groom

_____

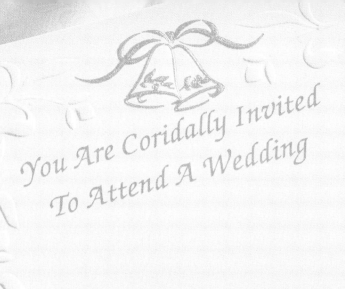

You Are Coridally Invited To Attend A Wedding

True happiness consists not in the multitude of friends, but in the worth and choice.

BEN JONSON

THE HONOUR OF YOUR PRESENCE

nce you have chosen your attendants, you and your groom can begin

putting together your guest list. Before long, you may realize that the

two of you have many more friends and relatives than you thought!

Creating your guest list is one of the most challenging tasks that you

will face while planning your wedding. Naturally you want to share

this wonderful day with your friends and family, but you also have to

stay within your budget. Planning your guest list can be an enjoyable

experience as you choose your guests with both love and care.

Your first step is to take a deep breath, get out a pencil and paper, and determine approximately how much money each guest will cost. Remember that you don't need a complete, finalized menu from the caterer to do this. Nor do you need your reception site to be confirmed. (In fact, final caterer and reception plans depend on the number of guests you decide upon.) Just estimate as accurately as you possibly can.

Err on the high side of your approximate figure. This is one of the most special events in your life, and while it's always good to be practical, you'll be cheating yourself out of a truly special day if you scrimp too much. Trust your common sense and family finances to guide you.

Decide on a number

Once you have an idea of the cost per guest, it is time to decide how many people you would like to help you celebrate. While you are brainstorming who to invite, begin with your families and work outward to your friends.

When you have an estimate of how many guests you would like (and can afford) to invite, it will help greatly to set up several different lists as you iron out the details. Try using the following as a guide:

The essential guests: This list includes immediate family, the officiant, and the wedding party.

The cherished guests: Although these people may not play a huge role in your actual wedding day, they form your circle of much-loved friends and family.

The necessary guests: This is your list of people who you *should* invite—namely, your extended families, as well as people whose weddings *you* were invited to and must reciprocate. The best way to navigate the terrain of the extended family is to decide on a cutoff—for example, "second cousins, once removed"—and to stick to it.

The guests from work: Decide together who from your respective workplaces you would like to come, and remember that bosses should probably be the first on the list.

The meaningful guests: You keep up an email correspondence with your dear poetry professor from college. Your groom credits his career as a musician to his first piano teacher. Consider inviting those people who have significantly touched your lives. They played a role in who you are today, and will make your celebration all the more precious.

While you and the groom compose your different priority lists, it's a good idea to keep the equitable division of guests in mind. Traditionally, the guest list is divided fifty-fifty: half for the bride, her family, and friends; and half for the groom, his family, and friends. Many people still use this simple guideline to create the guest list.

A more contemporary method of dividing the guest list is quickly becoming just as popular. Devote one third of the guest list to the bride's family, another third to the groom's family, and the final third to the bride and groom. This is especially useful when the two of you have a number of close mutual friends.

Paring it down

Once you have several filled-out lists in front of you, you may notice how very long they look! The following suggestions are meant to help you shorten them with grace.

Try not to make exceptions. Even if you're not close to one of your aunts, you should think of inviting her if all the other aunts are invited. Similarly, try not to make exceptions for that especially-loved third cousin if the other third cousins are not invited. (They may hear about it.)

Consider an age cutoff. At the reception, you may want your nearest friends to be able to celebrate without minding the children. A good way to set an age cutoff is to write "Adult Reception" on the response card.

Try to limit dates. If most of your single guests will know lots of people at the reception, you may want to limit dates to those of immediate family and members of the wedding party. Traditionally, the way to sanction dates on an invitation is to write "Shawna Casey and Guest"; the way to discourage them is to just write "Shawna Casey."

A friend let us in on a very successful way to visualize the guest list. He and his fiancée created a mock floor plan of the reception. Here's how to go about it:

- Start with your number estimate. Even if you haven't booked the reception site yet, you will know from this figure how many guests you plan to share your celebration with.

- Choose the size of each table: generally, anywhere from six to ten guests per table works best.

- Start filling in the tables on a sheet of paper. If you want the groom's friends from work at one table, the floor plan will let you see that there are three spaces left, and you can plan the remaining guests from there.

Each friend represents a world in us,

a world possibly not born until they arrive,

and it is only by this meeting that

a new world is born.

ANAÏS NIN

WEDDING GUESTS

Use the following pages to keep track of your confirmed guests.

Reproduce pages if extra space is needed.

name	no. in party
address	

name	no. in party
address	

name	no. in party
address	

name	no. in party
address	

name	no. in party
address	

name	no. in party
address	

name	no. in party
address	

name	no. in party
address	

_____ _____   _____ _____
name   no. in party   name   no. in party

_____   _____

_____   _____
address   address

_____ _____   _____ _____
name   no. in party   name   no. in party

_____   _____

_____   _____
address   address

_____ _____   _____ _____
name   no. in party   name   no. in party

_____   _____

_____   _____
address   address

_____ _____   _____ _____
name   no. in party   name   no. in party

_____   _____

_____   _____
address   address

_____ _____   _____ _____
name   no. in party   name   no. in party

_____   _____

_____   _____
address   address

_____	_____
name	no. in party
_____	
address	

_____	_____
name	no. in party
_____	
address	

_____	_____
name	no. in party
_____	
address	

_____	_____
name	no. in party
_____	
address	

_____	_____
name	no. in party
_____	
address	

_____	_____
name	no. in party
_____	
address	

_____	_____
name	no. in party
_____	
address	

_____	_____
name	no. in party
_____	
address	

_____	_____
name	no. in party
_____	
address	

_____	_____
name	no. in party
_____	
address	

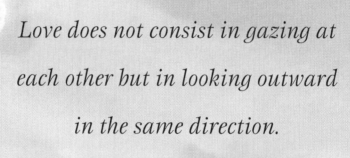

Love does not consist in gazing at

each other but in looking outward

in the same direction.

ANTOINE DE SAINT-EXUPÉRY

UNIQUE
INVITATIONS

A very important step is now behind you: you have decided upon your guests. But just as important as who you invite is how you invite them. Your invitation is the first part of your wedding day that your guests will see—for this reason, it should reflect the joy of the occasion, as well as the unique spirit of your wedding day. Inviting guests with style and grace means paying attention to the details: stationery, proper wording, and good etiquette. Start with these basics, add your own panache, and you'll soon be sending invitations that are perfect to the letter.

A wedding invitation can take many different forms, from a simple handwritten note to a formal embossed card written by a calligrapher's pen, complete with a response card and site maps. As a general rule, handwritten invitations are only acceptable if you're planning a wedding with less than 50 guests; otherwise, you may end up with a sore hand! For larger parties, enlist the services of a wedding stationer.

BRIDE'S HELPER

Don't be shy about providing detailed site maps for the ceremony and reception in the invitation envelope. The more information you provide at this time, the fewer phone calls you will receive as the wedding day approaches.

When you order invitations, make sure to order extra. Invariably, a few mistakes will be made in the addressing, or you may add some guests later. As a general rule, order one-quarter more of everything than you "officially" need; if your guest list has one hundred names, order twenty-five extra. Do the same for envelopes, maps, and RSVP cards.

What to say?

Most wedding experts agree that simplicity is key when wording your wedding invitation. Following are a few basic examples of proper wording, which you can change easily to suit your own occasion:

A Wedding Invitation

When the wedding is hosted by the parents of the bride:

Mr. and Mrs. James Duchamp
request the honour of your presence
at the wedding of their daughter
Julia Duchamp
to
Mr. Douglas Winter
on Sunday, the eighteenth of November
at two thirty in the afternoon
Reception and dinner immediately following

When the bride and groom host the wedding:

The honour of your presence is requested
at the wedding of
Kathleen Schultz
to
William Jackson
on Saturday, the tenth of March
at four o'clock in the afternoon
Reception and dinner immediately following

When the bride's and groom's parents co-host the wedding:

Mr. and Mrs. Jeremy Spurling
and Mr. and Mrs. Peter Adams
request the honour of your presence
at the wedding of
Candace Spurling
and
Joel Adams
on Tuesday, the nineteenth of September
at ten thirty in the morning
Reception and lunch immediately following

BRIDE'S HELPER

- *Request the honour of your presence:* This formal wording is appropriate for invitations to the ceremony itself, as well as for combination invitations to the ceremony and reception. Traditionally, it is used for more formal weddings, or weddings held in a religious institution. In this context, "honour" is always spelled with a "u."
- *Request the pleasure of your company:* This is used for invitations to the reception only. It is also the preferred wording for invitations to less formal weddings or those not in a religious institution, such as home weddings.

A special kind of invitation

The use of outer and inner envelopes sets wedding invitations apart from any other kind of invitation. An essential for any formal wedding, and a nice touch for a casual wedding, this double layer allows for a greater degree of intimacy with the guests. The outer envelope fulfills all of the functions of a regular mailing envelope: it includes the mailing address of the recipient, postage, and the address of the sender. The inner envelope will refer to the recipient(s) by name only, and is always left unsealed.

As well as the actual invitation card, you may want to include a response card in this inner envelope. Using this will allow you to better keep track of your confirmed guests. If you decide that this is a good idea, consider including return postage. It's a thoughtful gesture at a relatively insignificant expense.

Proper etiquette: The icing on the cake

Here are a few tips to remember when addressing your wedding invitations.

- Handwrite the full names and addresses of the guests on the outer envelope.
- Handwrite the full names and titles of the guests on the inner envelope.
- With the exception of titles (such as Dr., Mr., Mrs., Miss, or Ms.), do not abbreviate anything on any envelope, including addresses.
- If children are invited, their names appear only on the inner envelope of their parents' invitation. The parents' names alone appear on the outer envelope.
- If your friend Sally Brown is bringing a "mystery" date, write "Sally Brown and Guest" on the inner envelope, addressing the outer envelope to Sally Brown alone.

It is thought that the tradition of using two envelopes for weddings harks back to the time when mail was delivered by hand. For gentility's sake, the inner envelope was left unsealed.

Our Wedding Invitation

Blessed are those who can give without

remembering, and take without forgetting.

ELIZABETH BIBESCO

YOUR WISH LIST

A marriage is a celebration of your new start in life with the one you love. But there's a practical side to building a life together that involves more than roses and rings. You'll need a toaster oven in the morning, towels for the bathroom, fine china for family gatherings, and even luggage for the honeymoon. Luckily, no newly minted couple is expected to afford the makings of a new home together. It's become tradition that a bride and groom's community welcomes the newlyweds into their life with the giving of gifts.

So how do you avoid getting three coffee makers when you really need satin sheets? (Or vice versa.) The answer, of course, is the bridal registry—your personalized wish list. Your guests will rest assured that they have truly given you a gift you will appreciate and by which they will be remembered. At the same time, you end up well-equipped for your new home. Best of all, the service is free.

Registering your wish list

More and more stores are offering bridal registry services, so you should find ample choice as you start your search. There are now

even reputable registries online, which can make shopping quick and easy for you and your wired guests. Online bridal registries are also an excellent alternative to catalogue shopping for out-of-town guests. Remember, you can register at more than one store, but be careful not to duplicate your selections.

The bridal registry is a good opportunity to invest in finer quality items that will last through your marriage. Do remember, though, that you will still have to shop with a budget in mind—that of your guests.

BRIDE'S HELPER

Already have a full house and don't need another tea set or toaster? Registries don't always have to mean fine china and monogrammed towels. If you and your groom have been living together before the wedding, or this isn't your first trip down the aisle, consider alternative registries. You may want to sign up supplies for a new home office or register at a golf shop, museum shop, antiques store, or camping outfitter.

Choose a store that offers the items you want and need in a wide range of prices, from the luxurious to the practical.

Before making a decision, visit or call the store to get a sense of how helpful the staff is. Be sure to ask about delivery, gift wrapping, and return policies.

Register sooner, rather than later, and at least three months before the wedding. This will give your close friends and family time to politely pass the word around to inquiring guests, since registries are never indicated on the wedding invitation. Your guests will then have the time to shop at their convenience.

Keeping track of gifts

It's important to be ready to start keeping track of gifts from the engagement. Whether received at a bridal shower, delivered to your home, or given at the reception, gifts should all be recorded and described carefully in a log—in fact, we think this is so important that we have included one for you. Why? For one, you'll avoid the awkward situation of forgetting to thank someone for a gift. You'll also have an easier time getting through the stack of thank-you cards if you diligently note who has sent what.

OUR WEDDING GIFTS

Use this log to record your gifts, reproducing pages if you need extra space.

Sender	Gift Received	Date Received	Event Received	Thank-You Note Sent

Sender	Gift Received	Date Received	Event Received	Thank-You Note Sent

...there was a bright glimpse of the rosy flow of her neck, and from her ambrosial head of hair a heavenly fragrance wafted; her dress flowed down right to her feet, and in her walk it showed, she was in truth a goddess.

VIRGIL

A BEST-DRESSED WEDDING

*I*t may be that your wedding day has been in the planning stage

for more years than you can guess. Maybe when you were a little girl

you would lie awake in your bed, gaze out the window, and think

about a night wedding under the stars. Or maybe you imagined how

you would wear you hair. Tumbling down your shoulders, with flow-

ers woven in? A soft french twist with flowing tendrils? Would your

train be so long that three people would have to carry it behind you?

No matter what, one thing was clear: the dress would be magical.

THE PERFECT WEDDING GOWN

A dress by any other color...

Growing up, we learn that brides are beautiful and that they wear white. While it is true that a bride on her wedding day is indeed beautiful, it is also true that she wears whatever color she chooses. In China, brides wear red, the color of happiness. In Iceland, brides wear black. Let your own symbolism, color preference, and the time of year, guide you to make your wedding dress truly your own.

Fitting the dress

Experts advise that you begin your search for a wedding dress anywhere from six months to a year before your wedding date. Often it takes months to order the dress you choose and then, to guarantee a perfect fit, you'll probably want three fittings, usually three months apart, with the last fitting six weeks to one month before the wedding. The first fitting takes place once your dress arrives, the second fitting adjusts the first alterations, and the third is a final check. When you go for a fitting, be sure to bring the shoes you plan to wear—or at least shoes of a similar height and design—and to wear the undergarments that you plan to wear with your dress. This ensures that you'll have no last-minute fitting surprises!

> **BRIDE'S HELPER**
>
> Magic on a budget is possible. But budget roughly six percent of your wedding funds on the dress and its accoutrements. This six percent should also include the money you set aside for alterations to the dress.
>
> ---
>
> If you are getting married for a second time, it just so happens that, like first-time brides, you have your pick of dress colors and veil styles. While some encore brides have been advised not to wear white or veils, it is actually acceptable to do both.

Anne of Brittany was the first noted bride in modern history to dress all in white for her wedding, in 1498, to Louis XII of France.

FINDING YOUR STYLE

Have you decided on a formal wedding, a semi-formal wedding, or an informal wedding? What time of year is the wedding? From the ever-popular vintage gown to the more informal daytime wedding dress, start narrowing down your dress choices according to your wedding season.

Fall and winter weddings

A lovely autumn day or a lush winter occasion calls for a richer style than for a spring or summer wedding. Richer means more and fuller fabrics, and more textures—to match the feel of the season. For a daytime wedding, choose heavier fabrics but a simple style. Shy away from shiny trims, beads, and sequins. Evening weddings in the fall and winter, however, have no boundaries. Lush, rich, warm, decorative—all are in order. But for elegance, choose one or two design elements and stick to them. Consider a matching cape or jacket, trimmed in velvet or lace.

Spring and summer weddings

A daytime wedding in the warmer months translates to lighter fabrics and a softer look. Silk, crepe, or the classically lovely lace are all great options for a glowing (not flashy) dress. Consider lighter colors and lighter coverage. Bare your neck and shoulders—make the season yours!

BRIDE'S HELPER

Do you want your wedding to look spectacularly formal? A black-tie wedding might be right for you. In a black-tie wedding, all male guests are dressed in formal attire, as are the female guests. When everyone—not just the wedding party—is so superbly dressed, the effect can be truly dazzling. If you and the groom decide upon this, make sure to indicate it on your invitations.

She walks in beauty, like the night

Of cloudless climes and starry skies;

And all that's best of dark and bright

Meet in her aspect and her eyes:

Thus mellow'd to that tender light

Which heaven to gaudy day denies.

LORD BYRON

A beautiful veil

Veils, veils, and more veils—but how to choose? Bridal shop professionals recommend that whatever veil you pick, it should complement the style of the gown or dress, mimicking its length and picking up on its supplementary fabrics.

...and shoes to match

Most everyone has advice on the kinds of shoes appropriate for both comfort and beauty. The final shoe will most likely be a compromise between the two. For walking and dancing, a stacked heel or low heel will work best.

A hint of pearl, a flash of diamond...

If you are spending so much time finding your dream dress that selecting jewelry for your wedding day is becoming an afterthought, don't worry. It's actually better that way: your dress and jewelry should work in tandem to bring out your full wedding beauty. Your ring, of course, is the symbolic center, so plan the rest of your jewelry around it. The key is not to overdo it. If your dress has a lot of detailing around the neckline, it is probably best to forego anything but the very simplest of necklaces or pendants. Choose your earrings to complement not only your wedding ring, but also the hairstyle you have chosen for the big day.

The garter

The wedding garter, once used to hold up a woman's stockings, is traditionally worn on the left leg—closest to your heart. A lot of brides choose to build their own traditions around this wedding accessory: some borrow their garter from a happily married friend or pass down the garter generation to generation.

The impeccable groom

The groom is the man of the day and he stands apart, in his manner and certainly in his dress. His clothes, whether a tuxedo or a semi-formal suit, should have a unique quality that distinguishes him from the members of the wedding party. He may have a different vest from the men of the wedding party, a unique tie, or a distinct coat style—something that makes him stand out.

The groom follows the formal, semi-formal, or informal dress style you and he have chosen, and his suit or tux should offset your dress. Maybe his cravat matches the color of the flowers in your bouquet, or his boutonniere perfectly accents the ribbon in your hair. Your looks should complement each other as you stand together, dance together, and start your life together.

The wedding party

Your honor attendants are your close friends and family members and their clothing should reflect that bond. The wedding party should dress in a style that complements the attire of yourself and your groom, yet still distinguishes the wedding party from the wedding couple.

Style in collaboration

Traditionally, the bride has chosen the style and material of the bridesmaids' dresses and has arranged for them to be fitted to each woman. But body types are different, and what looks transcendent on one can look plain on another. A great solution is for the bride to specify the color and length of her attendants' dresses and let each choose her own dress according to her individual style. Some brides opt for separates, choosing the skirt and asking her attendants to purchase an elegant blouse of a uniform color. This way, honor attendants may be able to wear the clothing on other occasions. Luckily, dressing the groomsmen is usually not a problem, but make sure that their dress varies slightly from that of the groom.

While you may have chosen a dress simple enough that slipping in and amongst tables of guests is possible, you might want to think about changing into something suited specifically for the dance afterward. One couple we know hired a six-piece swing band to play at their reception. The bride and groom, who were accomplished swing dancers, did not want to be hindered by yards and yards of material. She changed into a simple silk skirt and top of a similar material and color to her wedding dress. She still stood out among guests, was comfortable enough to dance the night away, and was able to sit and visit with all of her guests.

The last-minute kit

Experts urge you to pack yourself a "Bride's Emergency Kit" for the day of the wedding. We've found that the following items are particularly handy on the big day:

- small sewing kit
- tissues, toiletries
- nail polish, nail file, extra pantyhose
- hard candy, packets of crackers, or protein bars (for snacks)
- hairspray (good for runs in hose too), brush, bobby pins

BRIDE'S HELPER

If you wish to preserve your dress in a pristine state for years to come, have it professionally cleaned as soon after the wedding as possible so that stains don't have a chance to set.

Baby powder is great to have along in case of spills on your white dress—just dab dress with water and then with baby powder.

Something old meant that the couple's friends would stay with them.

Antique jewelry, sew a piece of a vintage gown into the hem of your dress...

Something new is a look to the future happiness, success, and health of the loving couple.

Your dress, your lingerie, a wedding day jewelry gift from your fiancé...

Something borrowed is a token of the bride's family's love. To ensure good luck, the bride must return it.

Your dress, a piece of jewelry, a garter (better luck if it's loaned by a happily married woman!), a dress watch...

Something blue comes from the belief that the color blue represents fidelity and constancy.

Blue ribbon stitched into the hem of your dress, blue beads stitched onto your veil, blue ribbon in your hair, an engagement ring with a blue gem, a garter, a piece of blue lingerie...

And a silver sixpence in her shoe brings wealth to the couple in their early married life.

A sixpence can actually be obtained at a bank, but make sure that you ask for one several weeks before the wedding. Either carry this coin or have it tied into your bouquet with a ribbon.

The bride in her wedding dress

When words leave off, music begins.

HEINRICH HEINE

SWEET SOUNDS

*W*ho could imagine a wedding without music? As your guests wait

for your graceful entrance, they hear the beautiful strains of a string

quartet—or perhaps those favorite ballads that served as the back-

drop when you and your groom fell in love. And from the wedding

march to the last dance, music will guide you and your guests through

a day both solemn and joyous. This is why it is so important to choose

music that is really you, expressing all the love that has gone into this

wondrous day.

When it comes to your wedding music, your choices are extensive and distinctly personal. And as important a decision as what *kind* of music you play is *how* you play it. In short, you and the groom will need to decide whether to hire musicians for any part of the wedding day. Many couples choose a live sound for either the ceremony or the reception; to do so for both can become costly, unless you are lucky enough to have a talented musician in your circle of friends and family who is willing to donate a performance.

Also, live music will draw attention to itself; this can be an advantage or a detriment, depending on your wishes. If you want music to be strictly background to the flowers, decorations, and poetry of the day, you may want to consider using pre-recorded music at the ceremony, and a deejay at the reception. Conversely, a professional musician playing classical pieces can lend instant sophistication to your ceremony, just as a live band at the reception can reflect your own personal taste in party music.

> BRIDE'S HELPER
>
> When you speak to your band or deejay, you may want to discuss the volume level at which you would like the music played. It can sometimes be annoying when the music is so loud that guests can't hear each other over the music.

Such sweet compulsion doth in music lie.

JOHN MILTON

Setting the tone: the prelude

In classical music, a prelude is a piece that precedes a larger composition. In the same way, the prelude music at your wedding ceremony sets the tone of the upcoming event. As your guests enter the ceremony site, find their seats, and marvel at the beautiful flowers you have chosen, they should hear music that reflects the happy couple.

Usually, classical music is chosen for the prelude; however, if you and the groom share a love of another kind of music, consider playing that instead. One couple we know played the soulful ballads of Simon and Garfunkel as their guests arrived, and family and friends remarked that this choice really reflected the unity of the bride and groom.

You may wish to consider these pieces for the prelude:

- "Jesu, Joy of Man's Desiring" by Bach
- "Nocturne in E Flat, Opus 9, Number 2" by Chopin
- "Ave Maria" by Schubert
- "Greensleeves" performed by the Trillium Consort
- "Prelude to the Afternoon of a Faun" by Debussy

Here comes the bride: the processional

After your guests have had a chance to settle into their seats as the strains of your prelude music play, it is time for them to be awed by your big entrance. Processional music should accentuate the majesty of your presence. That short walk down the aisle is truly magical; it's the first time that guests (and, probably, your groom) will see you in all of your finery, with your beautiful bridesmaids and cute-as-a-button flower girl. So choose processional music that will deepen the experience.

You may wish to consider these pieces for the processional:

- "Wedding March" by Mendelssohn
- "Wedding March" from *Lohengrin* by Wagner
- "Elvira Madigan" by Mozart
- "Canon in D" by Pachelbel
- "Air" by Bach
- "Rondeau" by Mouret

While papers are signed: the interlude

If there is a lengthy pause during the ceremony, as there often is for the signing of the marriage certificate, consider offering peaceful music for your guests to enjoy. Interlude music is usually similar in tone to that of the prelude.

You may wish to consider these pieces for the interlude:

- "Sheep May Safely Graze" by Bach
- "Ave Maria" by Schubert
- "Jesu, Joy of Man's Desiring" by Bach
- "Spring" from *The Four Seasons* by Vivaldi

The first music you will hear as husband and wife: the recessional

Where the prelude and interlude music is peaceful and the processional piece grand, the recessional music is joyous above all. Select a piece that, to you and the groom, expresses sheer jubilation. After all, it is the musical accompaniment to your first triumphant minutes as husband and wife.

You may wish to consider these pieces for the recessional:

- "Ode to Joy" by Beethoven
- "Trumpet Voluntary" by Clarke
- "Rondeau" by Mouret
- Selections from "The Water Music Suite" by Handel
- "Trumpet Fanfare" by Mouret

As the guests file out: the postlude

While your wedding guests wait their turns to leave the ceremony site, playing postlude music is a thoughtful touch. Consider music from the prelude list.

In Egypt, the wedding march, or *zaffa*, is a musical processional with bagpipes, horns, drums, belly dancers, and flaming swords.

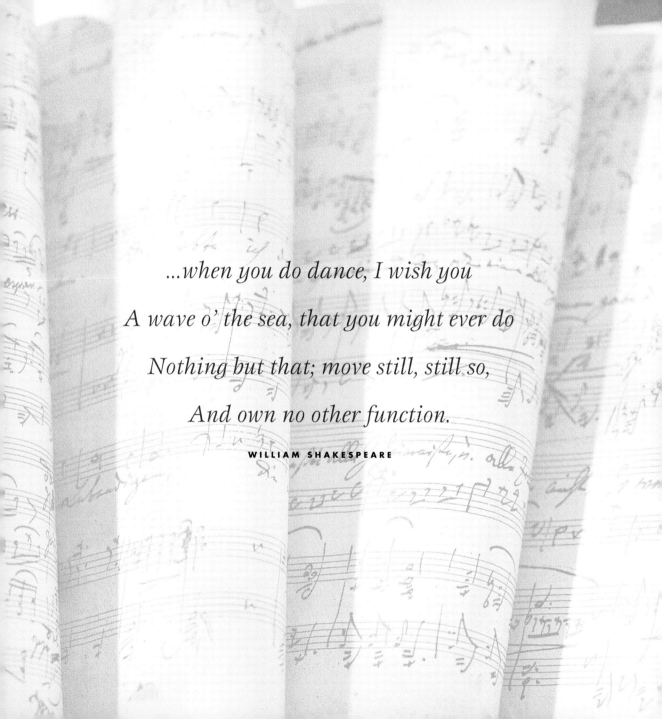

...when you do dance, I wish you

A wave o' the sea, that you might ever do

Nothing but that; move still, still so,

And own no other function.

WILLIAM SHAKESPEARE

Divine romance: the first dance

At your reception, the first dance will be one of the most treasured moments for you, the groom, and your guests. It is customary to choose a ballad that means something to you and the groom. If you have your own song—perhaps one that you first danced to, or the song that the groom put on the stereo before he proposed—by all means play it. It will make the dance all the more memorable.

If you and the groom don't already have a suitable song in mind, start listening to ballads in the genre of music that you like. The lyrics of some classic jazz ballads are timeless and absolutely charming; however, the same can be said of some more popular ballads. Whatever you choose, it should reflect the special romance shared by the two of you.

You may wish to consider these ballads for the first dance:

- "Somewhere" from *West Side Story* by Leonard Bernstein and Stephen Sondheim
- "At Last" by Etta James
- "You'd Be So Nice To Come Home To" by Helen Merrill
- "Can't Help Falling in Love" by Elvis Presley
- "Embraceable You" by Nat King Cole
- "When a Man Loves a Woman" by Percy Sledge

All night long: the reception dance

Whether you use a deejay or a live band, the music played at the reception dance should include the songs that will make the party a real celebration for you and the groom. Speak to the deejay or musicians about the style in which they play, the kinds of songs that are standards for them, and the songs that are musts for you. Also, ask them whether they plan to take breaks, and if so, the number and duration of the breaks.

It's a nice touch to keep the age range of your guests in mind. If you and the groom are big fans of contemporary pop, that's wonderful, but you may also want to include some older tunes, perhaps some Motown or Elvis Presley, as well as some classic ballads by Frank Sinatra or Louis Armstrong. This will ensure that you include older guests in the celebration. Another nice way to take the interests of your guests into account is to place request cards at each table.

OUR WEDDING MUSIC

Our prelude music is: _____

_____

_____

Our processional music is: _____

_____

Our interlude music is: _____

_____

_____

Our recessional music is: _____

_____

Our postlude music is: _____

_____

_____

Our first dance is: _____

_____

Our musicians are: _____

_____

_____

Our deejay is: _____

_____

_____

Memorable moments: _____

_____

_____

_____

_____

Like the brushing of swallows' wings

against the willows—sweet, sweet music!

LOUISE CRANE

So man did eat angels' food.

THE BOOK OF COMMON PRAYER

THE WEDDING
FEAST

*F*rom the most intimate get-together to the most lavish party, a sumptuous feast is the centerpiece of the wedding celebration. Throughout history and all over the world, the newly-married couple has always sat down with family and friends to a joyous meal full of the most extravagant and mouth-watering dishes that the culture has to offer. As you plan your own nuptial feast, think of your very favorite things to eat, and serve these dishes. If your wedding dishes are inspired, so too will be your celebration.

This will probably be a very simple decision for you, borne of the size of your guest list and the time of the reception. If the reception falls in the mid-afternoon or late evening, you will not be required to serve a full meal to your guests. If your food budget is tight, choosing these reception times will grant you the most grace on a shoestring.

Setting your own food style

Just as important as *what* you serve to your guests is *how* you serve it. Here are some serving options to choose from:

The buffet. In a buffet-style meal, guests line up to be served and are usually given two or three options for each dish. This can be a very good system when it comes to the degree of choice offered to the guests; it is especially helpful when you know that some of your guests are vegetarian, for example.

The seated meal. At a seated meal, the guests stay at their tables and the meal is served to them, course by course. If you have few guests with special diets, or if you have chosen a menu that will suit everyone, this is a sophisticated way to dine. A seated meal takes much longer than the other options, so if you want a stately pace to your wedding feast, this is the way to go.

> **BRIDE'S HELPER**
>
> If you choose a buffet, make sure that you pick a caterer who is experienced with preparing and executing successful buffets. Also consider inviting your guests to the buffet table by table: this will avoid long lines.

Food stations. An increasingly popular choice at weddings, food stations are a kind of modernized buffet in which "stations," or food tables, are scattered about the reception room, each with a different theme. A single reception could have, for example, a pasta table, a sushi bar, a meats table, a vegetable table, and a fruit table, allowing guests to sample foods as they like. That way, you can avoid long line-ups while giving guests a chance to mingle.

Cocktails and hors d'oeuvres. This is an elegant choice for a late-evening reception—and, if you choose lots of different finger foods, it will be quite satisfactory for hungry guests as well. The hors d'oeuvres can be brought around to the guests by wait staff, or they can be served buffet-style.

Elaborate wedding feasts are common throughout history. Viking wedding feasts usually lasted a full month, and, in Jewish tradition, the bride and groom would take a brief rest before facing the gastronomic demands of their massive nuptial feast!

HAVE YOUR CAKE — AND EAT IT, TOO

The tradition of tiered wedding cakes comes from the old English practice of modeling the cake after the spire of Saint Bride's Church, London. In the last decade, however, wedding cakes have become as diverse as the bridal couples who choose them. The old standards are being abandoned for more personal varieties. Generally, the only real requirement for the wedding cake is that it be sturdy enough to support however many tiers you would like. For this reason, pound cakes are a popular choice, and they can come in virtually any flavor you can dream up.

Once the flavor of the cake has been decided, you have a full range of choices regarding shape (from round to heart-shaped to octagonal) and color of icing (the traditional white is being challenged by light pastels). Decorations are also becoming more creative and adaptable to the unique personality of the couple. Consider these different approaches to wedding cake decoration:

- Having your cake "monogrammed" with your new initials in icing
- Adorning the cake top with a throwaway bouquet (make sure your flowers are edible!)
- Decorating the cake entirely in edible flowers, such as pansies or violets
- Using a non-traditional cake topper, such as candied butterflies or marzipan fruit, or a symbol of a shared interest, such as a pair of miniature bicycles or tennis rackets

The wedding cake originated in Roman times, when a wheat cake was broken over the bride's head. The crumbs that fell symbolized good luck and fertility.

For good luck, every guest has to eat from the wedding cake. It is also rumored that single women who take a piece home and put it under their pillow will dream of their future husbands.

In the Caribbean islands, the traditional wedding cake is a rich, dark fruitcake, made of a full pound each of flour, glacé cherries, butter, raisins, prunes, and other dried fruits, and a dozen eggs. The fruits are soaked in rum anywhere from two to six months before the cake is made.

The Danish wedding cake is a marzipan ring cake, also known as the "Cornucopia Cake." The ring is filled with the sweetest things in life, including candies, fresh fruit, and sometimes sorbet.

In Bermuda, wedding cakes are topped with a tiny sapling. This is to be planted by the newly-weds at their new home, so that they can watch the tree grow as their marriage grows.

In the Ukraine, the wedding cake is actually a sacred bread called "Korovai," which is decorated with motifs representing eternity and the eternal union of two families.

Tradition says that to ensure a lasting marriage, newlyweds should save the very top tier of the wedding cake to serve at their first anniversary.

Our Wedding Cake

Our Wedding Menu

The forward violet thus did I chide:

Sweet thief, whence didst thou steal thy sweet that smells,

If not from my love's breath? The purple pride

Which on thy soft cheek for complexion dwells

In my love's veins thou hast too grossly dyed.

The lily I condemned for thy hand,

And buds of marjoram had stol'n thy hair;

The roses fearfully on thorns did stand,

One blushing shame, another white despair;

A third, nor red nor white, had stol'n both,

And to his robbery had annex'd thy breath;

But, for his theft, in pride of all his growth

A vengeful canker eat him up to death.

More flowers I noted, yet none I could see

But sweet or colour it had stol'n from thee.

WILLIAM SHAKESPEARE

THE BEAUTY OF
FLOWERS

Nothing makes a wedding more beautiful than flowers. Flowers are an integral part of the wedding tradition, from the bride's bouquet to the groom's boutonniere. They will enhance every part of the wedding, giving life, color, and style to both your ceremony and reception. Whether a single rose or an elaborate cascade of orchids, lilies, orange blossoms, and ivy, flowers will set the mood and reveal your own personality, making your wedding unique and solely yours.

The groom's boutonniere should be a flower that appears in the bride's bouquet. This tradition comes from a knight wearing his lady's colors as a display of his love.

There are so many criteria by which you can choose your wedding flowers. Color, texture, size, availability, and symbolism are some examples that you can use as touchstones. Your florist knows what flowers complement each other and work well with your ideas, so keep your florist involved in your discussions. You might want to select two or three main flowers for your bouquet or your decoration and have your florist recommend the foliage and other flowers.

Consider the following list of popular flowers when considering your flowers. A flower's special meaning may be important to you. Some flowers have special holiday associations you might want to incorporate: poinsettias at Christmas, daffodils and tulips at Easter, and wheat sheaves at Thanksgiving. Flower colors are also associated with seasons: blue and yellow in spring, purple and pink for summer, red and orange for fall and winter.

Flower	Color	Season	Meaning
Aster	Purple, pink, white	Summer, fall	Elegance, love
Azalea	Pink, white	Late spring, summer	Temperance
Bluebell	Blue, pink, white	Late spring	Constancy
Calla lily	Pink, white, yellow	Spring, summer	Magnificent beauty
Carnation	Many colors	Year round	Pure love, distinction, devotion
Chrysanthemum	Many colors	Year round	Wealth, abundance, truth
Daffodil	Orange, white, yellow	Spring	Regard
Daisy	White, yellow	Spring, summer	Sharing, innocence
Delphinium	Blue, white	Summer	Swiftness, lightness
Forget-me-not	Blue	Early spring	True love, remembrance
Gardenia	White	Year round	Joy
Iris	Blue, white, yellow	Spring	Health, wisdom
Lily	Orange, pink, white, yellow	Year round	Purity, innocence
Lily of the Valley	White	Spring, summer	Happiness
Orange blossom	White	Rare	Purity, fertility
Orchid	Many colors	Year round	Beauty
Rose	Many colors	Year round	Virtue, joy, love, beauty
Stephanotis	Pink, white	Year round	Marital happiness
Tulip	Many colors	Late spring	Love, passion
Violet	Blue, purple, white	Late spring	Faithfulness

SELECTING A FLORIST

A good florist will help you realize your dreams for beautiful bouquets and stunning arrangements, especially if you provide as many details about your plans as possible. Knowing the style, texture and color of your dress will help your florist suggest a bouquet that would best complement it. Other particulars you should tell your florist:

- The date of the wedding
- The location of the ceremony
- The location of the reception
- Your color scheme

Bring photographs of your ceremony and reception sites for your florist to examine. If possible, also bring a swatch of a bridesmaid's dress and photographs of it and your wedding gown. You should also bring pictures of bouquets and

arrangements that you like — these give your florist an idea of the style you have in mind. Consider the different types of flowers you prefer and have a backup in case the flowers you want will be impossible to get for your wedding.

Get recommendations for florists from relatives and friends, then interview two or three. Talk to each about your ideas, to find one who has similar tastes and can make both posh and practical suggestions. You can look at photos of the florist's previous work to see if it's a style you like. There are also florists who will arrange a full design of your wedding, including tents and lighting, so if those are your needs, you can have one person (or company) take care of it all.

PERSONALIZING WITH FLOWERS

From a single orchid to a cascading bouquet, flowers will help establish the style of your wedding. Your bouquet should complement your wedding gown, both in shape and texture. You might also consider ordering a floral wreath for your headpiece, or you can simply put sprigs of baby's breath in your hair.

Your bridesmaids' bouquets should be smaller versions of the bridal bouquet. The flower girl can have an even smaller version, or a basket of dried rose petals to scatter down the aisle.

The groom's boutonniere will be slightly different from his ushers' boutonnieres to distinguish your special man. Your parents and grandparents will also need corsages and boutonnieres.

You can also get flowers for other special people who help with the wedding. If your master of ceremonies and a helpful aunt have a boutonniere or corsage, your guests can easily find people if they have questions.

Use the following list to keep track of the flowers you've selected for all the people in your wedding.

Come live with me and be my love;

And we will all the pleasures prove.

CHRISTOPHER MARLOWE

Bride's bouquet _____

Flowers in hair _____

Flowers in the throwaway bouquet _____

Going-away corsage _____

Bridesmaids' bouquets _____

Flowers in hair _____

*Photograph of
the Bouquet*

Flower girl's basket _____

Flowers in hair _____

Groom's boutonniere _____

Best man's and ushers' boutonnieres _____

Ring bearer's boutonniere _____

Mothers' and grandmothers' corsages _____

Fathers' and grandfathers' boutonnieres _____

Other _____

_____

*Pressed Flowers
from the Bouquet*

Blest is the bride on whom the sun doth shine.

ROBERT HERRICK

PICTURE PERFECT

The person who eternalizes your wedding memories is going to be very important to you. Most couples agree that the memories of their wedding are just as important as the ceremony itself: with your friends and family gathered around you, you will be radiant. Your photographer or videographer will ensure that you treasure the mood for years to come.

Do you want sound and motion or do you simply want a variety of candid and posed shots? Many couples opt for both, though the theme or spirit of your ceremony and reception might make one choice more fitting than the other.

Videography

Videography is quickly emerging as a great way to capture your wedding day. Many couples prefer to have all the sounds and sights of their wedding day recorded. This also allows the videographer to interview the wedding party—documenting all the family and friends gathered in your honor. Professional videographers usually use at least two cameras and some use wireless microphones.

BRIDE'S HELPER

Wherever you decide to get married, you'll need to know if there are any restrictions on photography or video. Some places of worship do not allow filming (of either kind) during the ceremony, or they restrict it to a specific area. Remember too, that your photographer or videographer will need access to set up an hour beforehand. This is to get an idea of where things will take place, and what angles will provide the best light.

While it may seem that videography is expensive, there are videographers to fit every budget. You should request to see an actual taped wedding (complete with sound) rather than just relying on a company's promotional videos for enlightenment. You'll also need to ask about the editing process—and have some thoughts of your own on this issue. Usually, videographers will provide you with the outtakes from both the ceremony and reception. Based on their early conversations with you, they may decide to do a documentary-style film, a series of short "scene" shots, or a beginning-to-end recording with only a light edit.

Photography

Wedding photography, as a tried-and-true medium, has some established guidelines. Currently, two styles exist: photojournalist and traditional. A combination of both will ensure that you have all kinds of wonderful moments captured on film. The photojournalist will focus on every conceivable event in your wedding day, nabbing candids and "true" moments, whereas a traditional photographer will compose photographs throughout the day, placing people, and making adjustments. The two styles can be very complementary: on one hand you have a shot of your ring bearer as he ducks his head out of the church trying to catch a glimpse of you, and then you have the photograph of you and your family on the church steps. No matter what their style, good photographers have charm and patience. They can handle all kinds of moods and emotions, capturing the best ones on film.

Photography is valuable, but the images it creates are priceless—so budget generously.

To love is to admire with the heart;

to admire is to love with the mind.

THÉOPHILE GAUTIER

SMILE!

Photographers give a few tips on how to look your best on the big day. Use makeup to define your lips and eyes, but stay away from sharp lines and heavy makeup, which the camera will pick up. If you decide to have a pre-wedding makeup session, carefully record those colors and shades that looked the best on you. You can then recreate them to make your wedding day one of effortless beauty. Most photographers will,

in fact, advise you to do a "test run" of your hair and makeup. Have someone photograph you so that you can decide which angles you like best or what adjustments you should make to your hair or makeup. Most important, though, is that you relax in front of the camera. Enjoy yourself. This will ensure that you look relaxed—and just as happy as you feel.

The sun is believed to be a symbol of fertility, and it was for this reason that Scottish brides-to-be would "walk with the sun" (east to west on the southern side of the church), then circle the church in the direction of the sun (three times for good luck).

THE FORMALS

Whatever medium you've chosen to record your wedding day memories, be aware that certain images are considered traditional must-haves. These are posed shots and include the following:

- Bride and groom together
- Bride and groom with honor attendants
- Bride with attendants
- Groom with attendants
- Bride and groom with all the wedding party
- Bride and groom and both groups of parents
- Bride with her parents and/or stepparents
- Groom with his parents and/or stepparents
- Bride and groom with each family (including all siblings, spouses, grandparents, and children)

Another choice you have is whether to take your posed photographs before or after the ceremony. Many photographers advise taking them before the ceremony to ensure that everyone looks fresh. Then when the time comes for the reception, you and your groom won't miss a single minute with your family and friends. Some couples, however, would rather that the groom sees his bride for the first time as she walks down the aisle. Either way, his heart will pound at the sight of you, so the choice is yours entirely.

There is nothing nobler or more admirable

than when two people who see eye to eye keep

house as man and wife, confounding their enemies

and delighting their friends.

HOMER

PRE-WEDDING
PARTIES

*P*re-wedding parties are not just an occasion for gift giving. They're also a wonderful opportunity to introduce your closest friends and family members to one another before your wedding. Bridal showers, bachelorette parties, and the rehearsal dinner are a time for laughter and best wishes from your loved ones.

Bridal showers were first thrown for brides whose families were unable to put together a proper dowry. The bride's generous friends "showered" her with gifts so that she had a more tempting trousseau to take to her groom. Today, shower gifts still help the bride to stock her new household. While the bride socializes with old friends and cherished family, she is "showered" with love and attention.

The maid of honor is traditionally responsible for hosting the bridal shower, with the help of the bridesmaids. Good friends of the bride may also choose to host a shower—but the guest lists for each should be different so that no one will feel obligated to bring two separate gifts.

Shower games

Parlour games are a traditional element of bridal showers. They may be entertaining, poignant, or just plain silly—but games are a fun way for guests to break the ice and get to know each other.

Ribbon bouquet: As you open your gifts, collect the ribbons and bows and create a bouquet to carry at the wedding rehearsal. According to folklore, the number of ribbons the bride breaks while opening the gifts is the number of children she will have.

Marriage recipes: On recipe cards, ask guests to write down their recipe for a happy marriage—and be creative. Read the recipes aloud and try to guess who wrote them.

Dating game: Give the guests a list of questions about the bride and groom—such as, "When was your first kiss?"—and ask them to fill in the answers. Then quiz the bride. Whoever gets the most answers right wins a prize.

Photo album: Ask each guest to bring a photograph of herself and the bride, and share the story behind it. Buy a special album for the occasion and paste the photos in it.

Theme showers

Theme showers set the tone of a party and can inspire some of the most original, useful, and sometimes comic gifts. Here are some of the most popular themes for showers.

Round-the-clock shower: Each guest is given a time slot on the clock and brings an appropriately "timed" gift. For instance, a nine o'clock a.m. gift may be a new coffee maker. Lingerie is a favorite pick with guests who are assigned an evening hour.

Kitchen klatch: Perfect for both the aspiring gourmet and the clueless cook, kitchen klatches equip the bride's new kitchen. Each guest brings a recipe, along with any cookware or appliances needed to whip it up.

Pot luck: Guests are each assigned part of the meal to bring in a special vessel. After dinner, the casserole dishes, glasses, plates, and bowls are washed and become presents for the bride.

Gadget shower: This shower will stock the home with those essential electrical gadgets. Guests can bring electric alarm clocks, blenders, shower radios, or a power drill!

Bachelorette party

Why should grooms have all the fun? More and more brides are having their own version of the stag party.

Spice up a night on the town—the traditional format for a bachelorette party—by choosing a different atmosphere for each stop. Move from a hot dance club to a swank cocktail bar to a mellow jazz lounge. Finish the night at a pub where you can squeeze into a booth with your friends to share your stories of "Remember when?"

> BRIDE'S HELPER
>
> Many couples are now choosing to celebrate together with a "Jack and Jill" shower. This is a fun and casual way to share the traditions of a shower with both your male and female friends. You might want to throw a cocktail party or a backyard barbeque with theme-related gifts.

BRIDAL SHOWER

Date: _____   Location: _____

Hosts: _____

Guests:

_____   _____

_____   _____

_____   _____

_____   _____

_____   _____

_____   _____

_____   _____

_____   _____

_____   _____

_____   _____

_____   _____

Special Memories:

_____

_____

_____

_____

_____

Date: _____   Location: _____

Hosts: _____

Guests:

_____   _____

_____   _____

_____   _____

_____   _____

_____   _____

_____   _____

_____   _____

_____   _____

_____   _____

_____   _____

_____   _____

_____   _____

Special Memories:

_____

_____

_____

_____

_____

The rehearsal dinner is more casual and intimate than the wedding reception. It's a time for the participants in the wedding to relax and get to know each other, now that the planning and practicing is over.

The rehearsal dinner is traditionally hosted by the groom's family after the wedding rehearsal, on the night before the actual ceremony. The guests include the wedding party, the immediate families of the bride and groom, and any out-of-town guests. Other close friends and family members may also be included.

In the early 1800s, the bride's family gave a feast on the day of the wedding, and the groom's family gave a breakfast the day after, called the "infare." The rehearsal dinner is today's version of the traditional infare.

We love because it's the

only true adventure.

NIKKI GIOVANNI

True it is that marriages be done in heaven

and performed on earth.

WILLIAM PAINTER

CEREMONY
CELEBRATIONS

he wedding ceremony is the main event around which all of the other parties and functions—showers, rehearsals, reception—revolve. It is the fulfillment of that romantic proposal that still makes you swoon when you think about it. And most importantly, it is the rite that truly joins you and the one you love, in the presence of your families and friends.

YOUR NEAREST AND DEAREST:
THE SEATING PLAN

In many ways, where you have your guests sit will depend upon the number of family members and friends in attendance, as well as your own personal wishes. However, you may want to keep these traditions in mind.

In Christian ceremonies, the bride's family and friends sit on the left-hand side (as you face the altar), and the groom's on the right-hand side. The parents of the bride and groom should be seated in the first row on their respective sides.

In Jewish ceremonies, the parents of the bride and groom stand

under the chuppah. The bride's guests sit on the right-hand side, and the groom's on the left.

In both kinds of ceremonies, the following general seating rules apply. Siblings and grandparents are seated in the second row (or the first in a Jewish wedding), with the rest of the family in the next few rows back. If you would like a certain number of rows reserved for family, use ribbons, garlands, or flowers as pew markers. Other guests are seated from front to back as they arrive.

A GRACEFUL ENTRANCE:
THE PROCESSIONAL

Who would you like to join you in your walk down the aisle? No matter what the "rules" are for processional order, this is the question that you should really answer for yourself when planning your breathtaking entrance. Consider the following traditions as you plan the processional, but let your own allegiances guide you.

In traditional Christian services, the bride's mother is seated by an usher after all of the other guests have been seated. Once she is seated, the processional may begin. The officiant waits at the altar, with the groom and best man or groom's honor attendant standing to the officiant's left. Here is the traditional order of the procession:

1. Ushers (in pairs)
2. Bridesmaids (individually if there are less than four; in pairs if more than four)
3. Maid of honor/bride's honor attendant
4. Ring bearer and flower girl (together or separately)
5. Bride and her father (or other escort)
6. Pages (to carry your train, if necessary)

In a Jewish ceremony, the processional order can depend somewhat on formality and degree of orthodoxy. In general, though, the following order is accepted for the processional:

1. Cantor
2. Rabbi
3. Bride's grandparents (if formal; if not, they may already be seated)
4. Groom's grandparents (see above note for bride's grandparents)
5. Ushers (in pairs)
6. Best man/groom's honor attendant
7. From left to right (facing chuppah): groom's father, groom, and groom's mother
8. Bridesmaids (individually if there are less than four; in pairs if more than four)
9. Maid of honor/bride's honor attendant
10. Ring bearer and flower girl (together or separately)
11. From left to right (facing chuppah): bride's father, bride, and bride's mother

THE JUBILANT COUPLE:
THE RECESSIONAL

Chances are that you and the groom will be so starry-eyed during this short walk back up the aisle that you won't remember much! Nonetheless, there is the proper recessional order to keep in mind. Essentially, it is the reverse of the processional order, with a few modifications.

In a Christian ceremony, the following recessional order is customary. In all cases in which a male-female couple walk up the aisle, the female takes the male's right arm:

1. The bride and groom together
2. Pages to carry bride's train, if necessary
3. The flower girl and ring bearer together
4. The maid of honor/honor attendant and best man/honor attendant together
5. The bridesmaids and ushers in pairs (extras may walk together or individually)

In a Jewish ceremony, the following recessional order is customary. In all cases in which a male-female couple walk up the aisle, the female takes the male's left arm:

1. The bride and groom together
2. The bride's parents together
3. The groom's parents together
4. The flower girl and ring bearer together
5. The maid of honor/honor attendant and best man/honor attendant together
6. The bridesmaids and ushers in pairs (extras may walk together or individually)
7. The cantor and rabbi together, with the cantor on the rabbi's left

As times change, so too has the way we look at marriage. In the past decade, more and more couples have chosen to personalize their vows, enhancing the traditional wedding script—or substituting it altogether—with words and phrases closer to their own hearts.

Perhaps the lyrics of a particular song, when spoken, give you a particular thrill. Or perhaps a certain poem encapsulates all the love you feel for each other. Whether you use someone else's words, or write your own, personal readings and vows can make the ceremony very touching and beautiful. When you speak with your officiant before the wedding, ask about the possibility of using your own vows or including readings that you would like.

BRIDE'S HELPER

The perfect readings for your wedding ceremony can come from almost any source, whether poetry or prose, a sonnet or a speech from history. The only caveat: try to keep it brief. A short poem or paragraph is preferable to a page or more in length; this will help to keep everyone's attention focused on the words you have chosen.

Now join your hands,

and with your hands your hearts.

WILLIAM SHAKESPEARE

WORDS OF **LOVE**

Use these time-honored passages to light your way to a truly inspirational reading.

You were born together, and together you shall be forevermore.

You shall be together when white wings of death scatter your days.

Aye, you shall be together even in the silent memory of God.

But let there be spaces in your togetherness,

And let the winds of the heavens dance between you.

Love one another but make not a bond of love:

Let it rather be a moving sea between the shores of your souls.

Fill each other's cup but drink not from one cup.

Give one another of your bread but eat not from the same loaf.

Sing and dance together and be joyous, but let each one of you be alone,

Even as the strings of a lute are alone though they quiver with the same music.

Give your hearts, but not into each other's keeping.

For only the hand of Life can contain your hearts.

And stand together, yet not too near together:

For the pillars of the temple stand apart,

And the oak tree and the cypress grow not in each other's shadow.

Kahlil Gibran

You are my husband, you are my wife
My feet shall run because of you
My feet shall dance because of you
My heart shall beat because of you
My eyes see because of you
My mind thinks because of you
And I shall love, because of you.

Inuit Love Song

Let me not to the marriage of true minds
Admit impediments. Love is not love
Which alters when it alteration finds,
Or bends with the remover to remove.
Oh no! It is an ever-fixèd mark
That looks on tempests and is never shaken.
It is the star to every wandering bark,
Whose worth's unknown, although his height be taken.
Love's not Time's fool, though rosy lips and cheeks
Within his bending sickle's compass come.
Love alters not with his brief hours and weeks,
But bears it out even to the edge of doom.
If this be error and upon me proved,
I never writ, nor no man ever loved.

William Shakespeare

When two people are at one in their inmost hearts,
they shatter even the strength of iron or of bronze.
And when two people understand each other in their inmost hearts,
their words are sweet and strong, like the fragrance of orchids.

I Ching

Now we feel no rain, for each of us will be a shelter to the other.
Now we feel no cold, for each of us will be warmth to the other.
Now there is no loneliness, for each of us will be a companion to the other.
We are two bodies, but there is one life before us and one home.
When evening falls, I'll look up and there you will be.
I'll take your hand; you'll take mine and we'll turn together
to look at the road we travelled to reach this: the hour of our happiness.
It stretches behind us, even as the future lies ahead.
A long and winding road, whose every turning means discovery.
Old hopes, new laughter, shared fears.
The adventure has just begun.

Apache Wedding Blessing

Dear love, for nothing less than thee

Would I have broke this happy dream,

It was a theme

For reason, much too strong for fantasy,

Therefore thou wak'd'st me wisely; yet

My dream thou brok'st not, but continued'st it.

JOHN DONNE

Part of the reason why the wedding ceremony is so cherished, throughout the world and throughout history, is that it is a wonderful ritual. And no matter your religion or cultural heritage, you and the groom will probably want to include both well-established wedding rituals and your own personal touches.

Often, including a special ritual in your wedding ceremony is a reflection of your ethnic background, or an homage to past generations of your family and culture. It can make the difference between a beautiful ceremony and an unforgettable one.

The following are some examples of both modern wedding rituals and time-honored traditions.

Jumping the broom: During the times of slavery, African-Americans were not allowed to marry. Instead, they jumped over a broom in front of family and friends to the beat of drums to enter into matrimony. The broom symbolized the start of homemaking as a couple, as well as the joining of two families in helping with housework. Today, many African-Americans choose to repeat this ritual, either just before or just after they are declared husband and wife. Often, the broom is beautifully decorated and is kept as a memento.

The unity candle: In this ritual, two candles near the altar are lit, one by the bride's mother and one by the groom's mother, at the beginning of the ceremony. A third candle, between the two, is unlit. Either just before or just after being declared husband and wife, the bride and groom each take the candle lit by their mothers and together they use these to light the central candle. This popular ritual symbolizes the joining of two families into a new family.

Giving of coins: This is a traditional Spanish wedding custom in which the groom gives thirteen coins, called *arras*, to the bride. Thirteen is a symbolic number for the indivisibility of the wedded couple, and the giving of the coins represents the groom's commitment to support and provide for the bride. During the ceremony, the bride carries the coins in a special purse, or they are carried by a child attendant.

Breaking the glass: In this Jewish custom, a wine glass is covered with a linen cloth and placed on the floor by the best man at the end of the ceremony. The groom then stamps on it to cheers from the guests. Though there are many interpretations of this ritual, here is the one that is most agreed-upon: shortly after the destruction of the Second Temple in Jerusalem, a wedding celebration became extremely rowdy and exuberant. To sober the guests to the reality that their Temple was in ruins, a rabbi smashed a valuable vase in front of everyone. And so, breaking the glass represents the need to remember that, even during the most joyful times, the married couple must be aware that life sometimes carries difficulties.

Exchanging roses: Just before they are pronounced husband and wife, the bride and groom give each other a rose. The giving of a single rose means, to most people, the same three words: "I love you." The exchange of roses symbolizes the importance of these three words to carry the wedded couple through life. At each anniversary, the gesture is repeated, and the two roses stand together in one vase.

Apache sand ritual: Similar to the unity candle, this ritual symbolizes the joining of two families into a third. Three bowls are placed on a table near the front: one with colored sand, another with sand of a different color, and the third left empty. After the vows, members of the bride's family each take sand from the first bowl and put it in the empty one. Members of the groom's family take sand from the second bowl and put it in the first one. Then the bowl is stirred. Just as the two colors can never be separated, neither can the families.

OUR CEREMONY

Our Processional:

1. _____
2. _____
3. _____
4. _____
5. _____
6. _____
7. _____

8. _____
9. _____
10. _____
11. _____
12. _____
13. _____
14. _____

Our Readings:

1. _____ Read by _____
2. _____ Read by _____
3. _____ Read by _____
4. _____ Read by _____
5. _____ Read by _____

Our Vows:

_____

_____

_____

_____

Our Rituals:

_____

_____

_____

_____

Our Recessional:

1. _____   8. _____

2. _____   9. _____

3. _____   10. _____

4. _____   11. _____

5. _____   12. _____

6. _____   13. _____

7. _____   14. _____

Our Special Memories:

_____

_____

_____

_____

_____

_____

_____

Hail wedded love, mysterious law, true source

Of human offspring, sole propriety,

In Paradise of all things common else.

JOHN MILTON

RECEPTION READY

After an inspiring ceremony, the reception gives you and your guests the time to enjoy food, drinks, dancing, and—most of all— each other's company. It is a true celebration of all of the wonderful people in your lives, and the start of your new lives together.

The transition from ceremony to reception is best marked by the receiving line, the first chance you get to say hello to your guests and thank them for sharing the day with you. Some couples choose to greet their guests following the ceremony, and others choose to wait until they arrive at the reception site.

Either way, you'll have to decide how you want to handle the receiving line, and who you want to stand in the receiving line with you. Sometimes only the newlyweds greet, and sometimes they choose to stand with their parents only, leaving the attendants to mingle with the guests. Traditionally, however, the order of the receiving line from left to right is as follows:

- Mother of the bride
- Father of the bride
- Mother of the groom
- Father of the groom
- Bride
- Groom
- Maid of honor/bride's honor attendant
- Best man/groom's honor attendant

To avoid long line-ups and inconvenience to guests, keep your words short yet heartfelt. Greeting each guest graciously is as simple as making that guest feel welcomed with a sincere, "Thank you so much for coming."

For the feasting, conversation, and celebration that will take place, you will need to decide whether to let guests choose their own seating or to assign places to them. When choosing between an open seating arrangement and an assigned seating arrangement, keep in mind that you want your guests to he happy and sure of themselves. There are advantages to open seating (people can choose to sit where and with whom they please), but the drawback is that guests may feel unsure of where to go. Open seating can work very well for smaller guest lists, as there is less chance for confusion, and it can contribute to the intimate tone of smaller receptions.

For larger receptions, however, most wedding planners recommend assigned seating. Seats are assigned with place cards at each table setting, or labeled place cards can be picked up by each guest as he or she enters the reception. Arranging the seating can be quite enjoyable. It gives you a chance to seat people together who may not have met yet but would get along famously. Arranging your seating can also help you to seat those who are very shy at a table where they will feel welcome. The reception, after all, is all in the name of celebration. It's a great opportunity for the people who are close to you to be able to mingle with each other and enjoy themselves.

A few basic table groupings are as follows:

The head table: The bride and groom and the wedding party sit at the head table. Sometimes a very large wedding party makes for an unwieldy seating arrangement. In this case, the bride and groom may sit together at a "sweetheart table" just for two. This is set off in the center of the room, but is still near the wedding party table and the parents' table.

The parents' table: If parents are divorced and have new families, there may be two (or even three) parents' tables.

The special guests table: This table is usually reserved for the spouses or significant others of those in your wedding party. These guests also sit near the head table.

LET'S RAISE A GLASS...

You have said your vows, and now your friends and family can add their words to the joyous occasion. The best man is the first to give a toast, and the groom will usually give a toast directly following in which he toasts the best man, the bride's parents, and his own parents. After those two toasts, the bride may make a toast, followed by the parents and any members of the wedding party who wish to speak. Effective toasts are those that give a personal and touching story about the bride or the groom, or about the two as a couple.

Fun and games

Most everyone is familiar with the tradition of clinking your fork against your glass when you want the newlyweds to kiss. In some receptions, miniature bells are placed on every table to ring

in the kisses. There are, however, many variations on this classic theme. Some inventive wedding parties have provided the following examples.

Scavenger tables

Lists on the tables or a list read by the emcee will provide guests with a number of articles that, if found, will get the bride and groom to kiss. Items to be included on the list can be obscure or extremely easy to find, depending on the level of difficulty you choose, but the main idea is that for each item on the list (for example, a receipt from a certain store, a Florida driver's license, a paperclip) that a guest produces, the newlyweds kiss. To vary this game, some couples have extended the required kissing to members of the wedding party and their dates.

The "toast" in olden days was actually just that: a piece of scorched bread, used to soak up the (then very heavy) dregs of the wine bottle. When someone gave a speech, it was customary to raise the glass all the way to "the toast"—the original version of "bottoms up."

Win the table centerpieces

You've thought long and hard about the most beautiful flower arrangements. Why not share them with your guests? A few couples we know marked each table centerpiece with a number and had a lottery-style raffle to win them. You could also reward the winner of one of your games (maybe a little trivia contest or a sing-off) with a centerpiece.

How well do you know the bride and groom?

A really fun way to go about this game is to vary the questions about the bride and groom so that guests of all generations might be included. Questions range from the necessary "How did the couple meet?" to "What was Samantha's favorite popsicle flavor as a child?" The more amusing the questions, the more interesting the answers will be to close family members and more distant friends and relatives alike.

Putting tee—for a kiss

Golfing enthusiasts love this one! A small putting tee is set up at the front of the reception room and guests may try their hand at putting for a hole in one! Either the newlyweds kiss, or the putter gets a kiss from either the bride or groom.

Whether you have hired a band or a deejay, there are a few traditional and heartwarming dances to include in your celebration. It all starts, of course, with the First Dance, which is the dancing debut of the couple as newlyweds. Another lovely tradition is the Father-Daughter Dance. Cameras will flash at this dance, and after the dance has begun, the bridegroom may join in, dancing with his mother-in-law. As the music continues, other couples may slowly drift to the dance floor.

With a group of guests varying in age, the Generations Dance is a great activity. The emcee or deejay will have all couples move onto the dance floor and begin dancing. As the music continues, he or she will announce, "all those who have been married a year or less, please move off the floor." This elimination process will continue until you have the longest-married couple still dancing. For their accomplishments, you may want to greet them with cheering and applause, or present them with a celebratory bottle of wine or champagne.

O' the sudden up they rise and dance;
Then sit again, and sigh, and glance;
Then dance again, and kiss;
Thus sev'ral ways the time did pass,
Till ev'ry woman wished her place,
And ev'ry man wished his.

SIR JOHN SUCKLING

Cutting the cake

That most-photographed of all traditions is the cutting of the wedding cake. This practice hails from the belief that the cutting of the wedding cake symbolized commitment to share a household. For the cutting of the cake, you and the groom both hold the cake server as you make the first slice. The tradition then follows that you feed each other a piece of the cake. A bit of icing on the face is said to be the harbinger of a sweet and ever-rich life. But go easy, as too much icing can mean trouble in the future!

Throwing the bouquet and the garter

It's time to find out who's next to marry! It is a time-honored belief that the single woman who catches the bride's bouquet is the next to wed. Ask the single women to gather around you and toss the bouquet—but don't peek!

The same idea applies to single men in the throwing of the garter. The garter is a little more risqué: you sit on a chair while the groom takes the garter off your left leg, to many cheers from your guests. He then tosses the garter to the assembled single men behind him.

Your getaway

Time for you and your new husband to slip away from the party. Sometimes this is done as a big send-off, and sometimes the bride and groom simply wave goodbye as they duck away. You do not need to stay until the very end of your reception; in fact, you should leave before the party slows down too much, but after you have had a chance to dance and mingle with everyone who has come. Upon escaping, beware! A lively guest may have decorated your car for luck: those tin cans or loud chains are meant to ward off evil spirits.

Every gift of noble origin

Is breathed upon by Hope's perpetual breath.

WILLIAM WORDSWORTH

SAYING
" THANK YOU "

Your friends and family have dreamed with you, supported you, and planned with you. What better way to tell them how much that means than with a "thank you"? Writing wedding thank yous can be a daunting process: how do you express the gratitude you feel for all that your guests have done for you? However, a little guidance and advice from the experts can make your notes personal, heartfelt, and perfect.

TOKENS OF AFFECTION

To the wedding party

It is customary for the bride and groom to give thank-you gifts to all of their attendants. Sometimes the bride will present each of her attendants with a piece of jewelry to wear during the ceremony. Gifts for the groom's attendants can range from matching martini glasses to tickets to a theater, movie, or sporting event. For more ideas, consider the following:

For the women

- silk scarf
- certificate for a spa day
- journal
- personalized gift baskets

For the men

- bottle of vintage port or malted scotch
- an elegant monogrammed pen
- leather shaving case

For the children

- charm bracelet
- baseball glove
- classic children's book
- computer game or software

...and especially to the guests

It is a nice touch to give a little keepsake to the guests, a thank you for sharing the day with you. Traditional gifts can be small boxes of chocolates, votive candles and holders, boxed pieces of cake, small picture frames, miniature bottles of wine with personalized labels, or sachets of lace filled with potpourri.

Often used as wedding favors, candy-coated almonds are wishes for a happy marriage. They may be boxed in small packages or tied into string bags, and look almost like miniature precious stones!

WORDS OF THANKS

Thank-you notes are both simple and touching, and are a mainstay of wedding celebrations. If you would like thank-you cards that match your invitations, you should be sure to order them at the same time you order the invitations. All thank-you notes are to be handwritten, and for a personal touch, should refer specifically to the gift given.

Thank-you list organization

It is certainly easy for details to be overlooked amidst the buzz of your wedding plans. So put one of your trusted friends or family members in charge of looking after the wedding gifts, making sure that each gift card stays with the gift and that each gift card has the name of the gift written on the back. An easy way to keep track is to keep a copy of your invitation list with you and write down the gift received next to each name.

When writing down what people gave you, add enough details so as not to confuse one gift with another. You may receive five different platters, so drop in a word or two: "silver platter, rose design."

Thank-you note etiquette

It is important to be timely when composing and sending thank-you cards. Etiquette experts say that thank yous should be sent within two to three weeks of receiving a gift. Three months is considered the very longest you should wait, but the best plan is to have sent them all one month after your honeymoon.

Thank-you cards should go to all guests, all those who gave a gift, and all those who gave an item of theirs—such as roses from a garden. Also important are those people who provided their professional services, including the caterer, the photographer, and the band. It's wonderful to provide these people not only with words of thanks but with a tangible reference for their work in the future.

And yes, it is true: even if you give a gift or say thank you in person, still send a card: it has the power to make a person's day.

Formal:

July 29, 2002

Dear Mr. and Mrs. Gerald Bloom,

The ornate picture frame is beautiful. Such a practical and elegant wedding gift will be cherished for many years. It was wonderful of you to celebrate with us, especially having come all the way from Virginia.

Thank you so much.

Sincerely,
Alex

Informal:

September 28, 2002

Dear Bob and Jenna,

James and I really loved your gorgeous fruit bowl. We put it in our new apartment, and hope you'll come visit us there soon. Will you bring that lovely daughter of yours?

Can't wait to see you again! Thanks.

Affectionately,
Morgan

BRIDE'S HELPER

Writing thank yous as soon as a gift is received is recommended—even if you are writing notes before the wedding takes place.

For a wedding-shower gift:

January 9, 2002

Dear Gabriel,

It was great to see you at the shower last week and to hear all the news about little Sammy.

The silver platter you so generously gave us is the perfect gift, and is sure to be a lovely addition to our house.

Whenever Joseph and I look at it, we'll remember your kindness.

Love,
Tanesha

For those who were not able to attend the wedding, but sent a gift:

September 5, 2002

Dear Linda and Stan:

I cannot tell you how much we missed your presence at the wedding.

We'll have to visit in the near future and catch up.

As always, your taste in linen is impeccable. Thank you so much for the beautiful tablecloth! I hope to see you soon and thank you so much for your generous gift.

Yours,
Pam

WORDS OF THANKS

With all of your favorite people around you, it can be hard to keep track of the wonderful things everyone has contributed to your celebration. You also want to make sure you didn't miss sending anyone a card. Use this page and duplicate it as needed to record the gifts you received, as well as the dates on which you sent personal thank yous.

Name	Gift or Gesture	Card Sent

ABOUT AVALON MUSIC

Avalon Music is dedicated to producing the finest instrumental music. With a repertoire that ranges from timeless classical masterpieces through Big Band favorites, to upbeat contemporary jazz, we are committed to stylistic diversity, superb musicianship and the highest quality recording.

Other titles from Avalon Music include:

Also available from Avalon Music & Books:

For more information about Avalon Music and to see our entire catalogue, please visit our website at www.avalonmusic.com

Avalon